Rain Spells

Natasha Georgina Faiers

BookLeaf Publishing

Presentation by *BookLeaf Publishing*

Web: www.bookleafpub.com

E-mail: info@bookleafpub.com

ISBN: 978-93-95755-97-9

First edition 2022

DEDICATION

Poignantly to those whomsoever may need the engagement with some form of hope, relatedness and friendship. To Friendship.

Unconditionally you're loved.

ACKNOWLEDGEMENT

To the understanding loyal hounds of library
spaces and the wise owls of spiritual
enlightenment.
The small adventurers whom addressed my
mysterious with natural treasures and enjoyed
the quietude of solace in a music hall seat.
Thanks to all encounters large and small.

PREFACE

The story is about emotions, feelings the everydayness of interaction and relatedness. Many people are companion upon our journeys. Upon occasion the wider view is as mysterious as the portals which we look through to improve our understanding. It's oftentimes a personal drift to historic emotive sensitivity. A thunderglass of poured dialogue the narrative simple to listen too.

Introductions

I introduce myself as one.
It said tell more of what's about you.
I observed then plainly,
What came?
A garbled nonsense, yet it flowed.
Around the structure It confined,
More gentle was the late pasture,
bright the lamp which oils ancient shade,
creeping down the alley, dimpled.
What of it? The vision blurry,
the darkness clamped to high rumbles.
Challenged me to find a quell spot,
Distance is but seas away here.
Your own estranged enchanted land,
A moment from the night hurries,
Age speaks of long-ago flashes.

The Chair

No sill nor seat, no table laid,
Missing chatter absurd, profound.
Loosen the jaw and tell me more.
No lonely state, nor idle maid,
not ever hooves, since such mustard wade.
Flanks have rode, where long ago cloak's
swished prints,
The lamb, the feast, the ointment bread,
the spire, a few people, earth, sky,
the higher kind of true virtue.
Say more to this, my darling fair.
of what becomes in potters care?
The sand has weighed the grain, it's wash,
its window has found pixies peep.
The maritime of lore stays scattered.
My rigs, the web, the ribbon weaves.

Painting

Oh, such a picture and a crest,
The silk of all that carries hosts.
Barnacles the flight overhead,
the paddle catcher drip comes mead.
For when the gale it simpers low;
my wrote, my heart, my long betrothed.
Use sway upon the glistened hems,
of the wild another casting.
Sundews thrown with widgeon boot cuffs,
on the cobbled Streets of wet lochs,
Upon some sets of compass track.
Beyond adventure time then latched,
Sweep away the cobwebs dreaming,
inhale the deeper of divine,
for none hath known such tilting tides.

Seasons

Borne the sky it's constellations,
Within thickness of rudders thud.
So pure; the gentle breath breezes,
the balm of nightingale's the songs.
Belong the spray in tatters throng,
The melodious it claims thy ear.
My cruise a flagrant shining view,
a predator yet.
Clasp its sound soft,
It only has my mooring gaze.
Long as all has been in hulls, grace.
These barrel rolls of Brandy fine,
the lace of Venus in pursuit.
Such plums; the rouge cherry vineyard wines.
No, never say not you. I do.
Melt the seasons Chinked some mellow.

Springs In

Blossom drift, the bergamot sweet,
for belly my heart must take needs,
the question of attachment strengthened.
For courage not just muse but straight,
Fasten it with cane flair fondness.
Soulful in the visions dusting the tropical has
stirred such calm,
As the rain it stilled then carried.
Streaming it We wish it drove home.
Stand the point to quayside;
hasten.
My nocturnal calling oft stays
steps in port the morning rising.
Pretty town It drapes the landscapes,
Draws freshened colour to one's cheeks,
dotted jumbling across homeward.

Summer Pours

A moment, then it paused to filter,
Shore emerged with jangled lapping,
The porpoise hen like fin passed wide,
decrease the downpour tow swelling.
About the lark, the turtledove, Shanti guilded,
waking dawning.
Sea views nasal nostalgia.
Up again with gallops sea maids,
now circles shoal hubs, silver foams.
Turning heel to drift sturdy rafts,
Jump the sky burst, laden golden,
The tender warm give light today.
Rapture in the pleasure cornered.
Hefty. Clarity, devotion, adoration. The eyes do
speak.

Autumn Nest

Masters eye draw cup this splendour,
bring depth to more than raven lusts.
What holds the velvet trowel clipped dust?
No gallery can confine truth.
Might shattered through desert rock pools.
Flaying the soft opaque jewels;
gather closeness more than layers.
such as the sacred, freely kept,
Pava, glitter, rainbows, opals. You're Otherwise
traitors tread.
Mason can no way curve swollen,
from rack It strays to lean it's boughs,
never half more optimistic.
Ploughed out, softened, woven, blending;
only cradle loom rocks soothing.

Winters Light

Tell me only that of passion?
Oh, but what of kindred spirits?
Do not they understand of such?
The greater good, Unknown forces,
insights glean of pure gentleness,
of blushed peaches you're tenderness.
Sensitivity we must show
for long the heart has it bestowed.
Waited for the mindful reaching.
Was it for the conversation?
The interaction claimed it still,
of journey in the adventure.
How so? To later open gates? Forever is
redeemed indeed.
So tell my heart of what we see?

The Alchemy Crown

Behind the veils of just by chance,
what is meant is meant by passing;
so as in the travel to go on.
The moment of spontaneous,
the seldom pull of internal.
Wailing, It is not a banshee, not a boogie-lieu,
no, not ghost.
Core grounded inner sense, heartfelt,
intuition, the feelings.
A call of what feels the best thing.
For you will find those best things?
Some best things are meant for many times.
How can it be only this life?
In greater knowledge, to be sure, let's walk
together, then maybe more.

Twin Footprints

Where best would we walk our minds?
Along the galley, under vines, over mountains,
gentle foothills, round,
Cliff and mount, little churchyards, place and
grounds.
Tea and food they always matter.
For what flavours first should we taste?
So vast these lands of many folks.
The tiniest spider, Mews goats.
A goat? As milk and llamas, fleece?
Or leatherbacks a certain breed with wings and
kites of guarded knots,
Like trees stippled upon the crease.
Or sprouting mounds Sir loves a lot.
None will be without company,
So say you will journey with me?

The Room At Sixteen

I cannot see you here, so lonely.
May it learn us more of friendship.
Of understanding, can I ask?
What of you, how do you like me?
The open invitation placed.
Why the panoramic alters?
That you should moor up with request.
To wait the heat of the passage,
to what means this, you say patience.
It is the look in proper time!
Mute Swans would speak more of ventures.
They would fend off a bisons deer;
if it were for a lifelong mate.
Sometimes the silliness of it.
Ah, but then it sails calm waters.

Twenty One Bells

In the realm of what's before me,
in the place of longing, lovely,
Have that antelope steady pace?
Does the sky allow its glimmers.
The way the ice belt took shifting?
Hold iris lean upon shoulder; Look that
reflective, heiligenschein.
Come from the shadows let us see,
No encounter is forgotten.
The pleasure is engaging face to be the
ever-changing tone.
Knowing the truth is in the seeing.
Honest the heart is never blind,
So what is that deeper meaning?
To know a lifetime's expressions, love.

It's Cat and Dog

Of all things, the sounds to listen.
Do you hear the lap of the waves?
The wind breezing through the lagging?
The timid, far-reaching question.
Can you hear shy like coconuts?
The pause of clumsy feet, bean bags strewn
across the ocean paddling?
Miles away Pluto awakes.
The Moons Sea of tranquillity,
far into the great universe.
I hear anticipation like this?
Here and now, it's body conscious.
Reply to a skimming pebble, Neptunes son
would build a castle,
honey dogs just want fidget whiskers.

Remembrance Sheild

Sometimes elephants have hand hankies.
They the gentile knowing prairie horse.
The same would bring tea mountain top.
Like the unquenched bloom of legend.
Did it not spread its wings so wide?
Elusive woodsmen travellers
dappled woodside hilly caverns.
Coppice treasure May flowers sailing,
The lemon bathed sedge between streams,
for a wagtail a tender peck,
alive with darting southern chase,
Cage not it kept me ever yet.
Those wedgwood slopes, adonis blues,
Or aquamarines lovely hues for curiosity, long
adored.

A Calendar Day For Rain

Moon-fish, day-fish, night-fish, ray-fish,
Bays to hold cumulus, hope springs.
Beaver knows much lowed waters high,
Long gone penny dregs the Wharf cries,
Under the arches galloping hoof.
Might we travel together clear?
Water rippling decreasing levels.
Parched land somewhere sweet enough, please!
The sound of the rain welcome still;
The swirl of the teacup refilled,
puddles reflect the hazy rain.
Maybe we should anchor drop here?
Adventure places, recreational spaces, workout
through the asks, the maybes, stations, ports.
Where to places?
It's made it defined; more to do.

Life Jacket

The journey far from overboard,
the highlight seemed total assured.
We feel as though we met our match.
You're shown many things of beauty.
We also feel the deeper end,
the hearts longing sense of duty.
Some waved banners celebrating more.
Many can't understand the lost.
They say why weren't we doing more?
We steered. Sailed long. Docked harbor doors.
The shipyard our last lovely host. Pulled us from
the sunken deck boards.
Parked up tangled boys with ghosts.
Why?
It wasn't that we hadn't sailed enough.
Draining tides soon got too rough.

The Parasol It's Parody

A ferry house kept tavern fayre.
It led my love to you, my dear.
So broken nooks and torn page books,
the fonder love from friendship due.
I sat my towel acquaint full sail,
The Admiral would of being proud.
Sad it was padlocked. Understand?
The finest loved boat of all years,
unfortunate weather misbehaved.
It crept aboard. Then quite absurd.
A glassy world the paddler tiers;
Treasured the lovely friendship made.
The most enchanted of mine eyes;
A vessel for expressing life.
The finest, you're dearest darling.

Unknown Guest

More than lines upon this page,
sometimes the way to express it in accurate
ways.
The feelings;
when all is at a sideways glance,
then opt in the alternate route cannot be only just
by chance.
when it wrote the path.
It didn't then know my heart.

Mysterious True

19

One kiss to love you
A hand to lift you softly;
Together journey.

Journeys...
Hold on dear dreamer,
Starlight caress the lilac;
Mid evening rays.

Be-longing

Outside spindle branches curled as squirrel tails;
Brushing upon window with gentle tempo.
Wrapped in seasons embrace snug as merino
wool;
Lustrous favrile glass illuminates a shady corner.
Fragrant scented logs drift again;
Brisk clarnico air all the fresher as it sings.
Clusters of stars pronounced,
Jewels in the night sky pitch as raven's wings;
Porthole to distant galaxies astound.
Black cat's paws and little red dogs;
Hauntingly responded by music from a downy
owl.
Outsides world is turning with the leaves;
Brewing our wild instincts alertness.
Snowflakes first kisses melting on panelled
globe frames;
A sip of Cointreau warms dancing spirits soar.
Spinning each twirl star arms splayed like a Da
Vinci sketch;
Shakes of a snow globes mists twist.
Realisations we're together still of night
balancing its blend of attraction,
Settles softly with the mind;
Two dreamer's happiness in spontaneity called.

Quiet echoes cotton wool ears, heartbeats so
loud;
This is someone I truly love for keeps.
So sure that I heard the rhythm in the waves far
off at sea;
Lights shimmied ebb and tide simultaneously.
Trees swayed agreeing as they bent;
Yoga like breeze the secrets flushing winds.
Alive in this moment as stars peep and greet
each other.
Beautiful natures love surrounds;
Awoken sights, lost treasures found.
To cherish such heartfelt combined
completeness, Expressions rekindled as we read
each other like an old leather book;
Restoring my faith in romantic traditions
sweetness.
You're my true love story just waiting to
happen;
Unconditional you still belong!
Let's begin another chapter this is our song,
Co-ordinated kindred passion how it lingers;
Shall we nest here?
Turn the page, start over,
Could you stay my soul-mate my best friend my
lover?
For me there just couldn't be any other.

Your Love My Love

Your love is as some beautiful mythical bird;
That enchants my mind in glorious colours.
Your love is as some wondrous galleon;
That sails about my heart in drifts.
Your love is as a rainforest waterfall;
That quenches the souls thirst for knowledge.
Your love is like a painted butterfly slightly out
of reach;
That one day I hope in love to capture and
forever keep.
Your love divine,
Your love passion,
Your love soothes,
Your love mine.
My love is as a singing bird;
In sweet harmony with you.
My love is as a starry night;
In my zodiac I twinkle dream for you.
My love is as a garden;
That blooms each time we touch.
My love is as the blossoming tree;
That which nurtures all we love.
My love divine,
My love passion,
My love soothes,

My love yours.
Your love is as some wild horse;
This I imagine as I ride.
Your love is as a sailing kite;
This I hold as you so tight.
Your love is as a flowing river;
This glides so close with me.
Your love is as a sacred kingdom;
This sanctuary of my heart in which I do
believe!
Your love sweet,
Your love true,
Your love treasured,
For I do love you.
My love is as a shining light;
That illuminates for you.
My love is as a rainy spell;
That kisses fresh and new.
My love is as an inquisitive cub;
So cute and sweet like you.
My love it is a sacred space;
That longs for one love as you so true!
My love sweet,
My love true,
My love treasured,
If you will love me too.
For I will love you;
Cherish you forever.

I will kiss you;
Enjoy us both together.
I will hold you;
Wrap you safely in my heart;
For I will keep you with me not ever shall we
depart.